The Maltipoo Method

A Guide to Successful Dog Ownership: Master the Art of Raising, Training, and Caring for Your Maltipoo

Gus Tales

GUS TALES PUBLISHING

Copyright © 2023 by Gus Tales

All rights reserved.

No part of this book may be reproduced, scanned, or distributed in any printed or electronic form without permission.

This publication is designed to provide accurate and authoritative information in regard to the subject matter covered. It is sold with the understanding that neither the author nor the publisher is engaged in rendering legal, investment, accounting or other professional services. While the publisher and author have used their best efforts in preparing this book, they make no representations or warranties with respect to the accuracy or completeness of the contents of this book and specifically disclaim any implied warranties of merchantability or fitness for a particular purpose. No warranty may be created or extended by sales representatives or written sales materials. The advice and strategies contained herein may not be suitable for your situation. You should consult with a professional when appropriate. Neither the publisher nor the author shall be liable for any loss of profit or any other commercial damages, including but not limited to special, incidental, consequential, personal, or other damages.

Book Cover & Illustrations by Alrium Digital

Contents

Introduction	2
1. The Story of The Maltipoo Unpacking the Charm of This Hybrid Breed	5
2. Adopting Your Maltipoo Making an Integral Choice	14
3. Preparing for Your Maltipoo Creating a Safe and Welcoming Environment	21
4. Settling Your Maltipoo Managing the First Few Days and Nights	30
5. Maltipoo Puppy Essentials Socialization, Training, and Early Care	38
6. Maltipoo Training Fundamentals Positive Reinforcement and Essential Commands	45
7. Maltipoo Nutrition Ensuring a Balanced Diet	54
8. Exercise and Enrichment for Your Maltipoo	61
9. Maltipoo Health and Wellness Regular Check-Ups and Preventative Care	67

10.	Traveling with Your Maltipoo Ensuring Safe and Enjoyable Journeys	75
11.	Connecting with the Maltipoo Community Networking, Resources, and Advocacy	82
12.	Maltipoo Grooming Ensuring Your Pet Looks and Feels Their Best	89
13.	The Aging Maltipoo Navigating the Golden Years	98
14.	Maltipoo Q&A Common Questions and Concerns	105
15.	Maltipoos and Kids/Other Pets Ensuring Harmonious Relationships	114
16.	Emergency Preparedness for Your Maltipoo	122
Afterword		131

Introduction

Hello, fellow dog lovers!

Welcome to "The Maltipoo Method: A Guide to Successful Dog Ownership." My name is Gus Tales, the proud owner of Isabel, a 5-year-old ruby Cavapoo who fills my life with joy and companionship. Although I am not a Maltipoo owner, I have had the privilege of getting to know this breed intimately, immersing myself in the unique culture of Maltipoos, and I am thrilled to share this knowledge with you through this comprehensive guide.

In this book, my aim is to empower you with the knowledge and tools to navigate the rewarding journey of Maltipoo parenthood successfully. I have collaborated with a team of experts including cynologists, veterinarians, and specialists in canine behavior to bring you the most accurate and beneficial information possible. This guide reflects a comprehensive and holistic approach to Maltipoo ownership, thanks to the vast knowledge and experience of these experts.

The following chapters will provide in-depth information on all aspects of Maltipoo care, from their history and unique traits to the essential practices and routines that ensure a harmonious co-existence. This guide will walk you through choosing the perfect puppy or adopting a Maltipoo from a rescue organization, preparing your home, establishing routines, and building a strong, loving bond with your new canine companion. We'll also explore the unique rewards and challenges of senior Maltipoo care, including appropriate diet, medical care, grooming, training, physical activity, and mental stimulation.

We will also examine the broader Maltipoo community, including clubs, events, and online and offline resources that can enrich the experience of owning a Maltipoo. This network of fellow enthusiasts will provide a wealth of inspiration, advice, and camaraderie as you journey with your cherished Maltipoo.

As you embark on this exciting journey with your Maltipoo, remember the importance of love, patience, and consistency at all times. These qualities will not only deepen your bond with your dog but also pave the way for a lifetime of happiness and understanding.

Together, let's embark on this amazing journey, and I wish you and your Maltipoo a lifetime of joy, amusement, and companionship. Welcome to "The Maltipoo Method."

Sincerely,
Gus Tales & Isabel the Cavapoo

CHAPTER 1

The Story of The Maltipoo
Unpacking the Charm of This Hybrid Breed

The Origin and History of the Maltipoo

Welcome to the enchanting world of Maltipoos, where the cuteness quotient overflows, and love, loyalty, and companionship come bundled in a pint-sized package. This popular hybrid breed, a delightful mix of the Maltese and Poodle, has rapidly gained popularity over the past few decades, thanks to their endearing personalities and minimal shedding coats—a big plus for allergy sufferers!

The story of the Maltipoo's origin is a relatively recent one. Unlike ancient breeds, whose histories date back thousands of years, the Maltipoo is a modern creation, first bred intentionally in the United States in the late 20th century. Breeders were seeking to combine the Maltese's charming and affectionate nature with the Poodle's renowned intelligence and hypoallergenic coat. The result was an instant success—these pint-sized pups stole the hearts of dog lovers everywhere, making them a beloved staple in the world of designer dogs.

> **Fun Fact:** Did you know the Maltipoo is part of the "Doodle" trend, which started in the late 1980s when breeders first crossed Poodles with other breeds to create hypoallergenic guide dogs?

Understanding Breed Designations: F1, F1b, F2, and Beyond

As we delve further into the world of Maltipoos, you'll come across terms like F1, F1b, and F2. These designations indicate the specific generation of the Maltipoo and can give you a hint about the pup's potential characteristics.

- **F1 Maltipoos** are first-generation pups, meaning they have a Maltese parent and a Poodle parent. These pups tend to exhibit a nice blend of both breeds' traits and typically have a wavy coat that's low-shedding.

- **F1b Maltipoos** are a backcross, with one F1 Maltipoo parent and a purebred Poodle or Maltese parent. This breeding typically aims to enhance certain traits, like the hypoallergenic coat or specific size.

- **F2 Maltipoos** are second-generation dogs, resulting from the mating of two F1 Maltipoos. The characteristics of these pups can be less predictable, as the genes from the original Maltese and Poodle can combine in various ways.

Remember, the breed designation isn't a quality stamp or a predictor of the pup's temperament—it's a tool that helps potential owners understand the pup's genetic background.

Tip: If you have specific needs, such as a hypoallergenic dog or one of a certain size, working with a reputable breeder who understands these breed designations can help ensure you're adopting a pup that will be a good fit for your family.

Unpacking the Physical Traits of Maltipoos

Now let's explore the captivating physical attributes that make Maltipoos such a hit among dog lovers. One look at a Maltipoo, and it's easy to see why they're often described as teddy-bear-like—they are adorably cute and snugly!

Size, Coat Types, and Color Variations

Maltipoos are small dogs, typically weighing between 5 and 20 pounds (2.3 to 9 kg), and standing about 8 to 14 inches tall (20 to 35 cm). Remember, the size can vary widely depending on the size of the Poodle parent—Toy, Miniature, or Standard. Most Maltipoos are bred with Toy or Miniature Poodles, keeping them in the small to medium size range.

Their coat, a charming legacy of their Poodle parentage, ranges from wavy to curly and is soft to the touch. It's also considered hypoallergenic, which means it's less likely to cause allergic reactions. Keep in mind, though, that no dog is 100% hypoallergenic—it's just that some breeds produce fewer allergens than others.

Maltipoos come in a variety of colors, from pure white to black and many shades in between, including cream, apricot, silver, and even multi-color or phantom, which means they have distinct color markings. The coat color can change as the dog grows and matures, so don't be surprised if your pup's coat lightens or darkens over time—it's all part of the Maltipoo magic!

Exploring the Maltipoo's Intelligence and Temperament

Beyond their adorable looks, Maltipoos have plenty to offer. They're intelligent, lively, and affectionate, making them fantastic companions.

As descendants of the Poodle—one of the most intelligent dog breeds—Maltipoos are quick learners. They're agile and can excel in dog sports like agility and obedience. Training your Maltipoo can be an enjoyable and rewarding experience. Remember, a mentally stimulated Maltipoo is a happy one!

Maltipoos are also known for their loving and gentle nature, inherited from their Maltese parent. They form strong bonds with their families and are particularly good with children and other pets. Their friendly demeanor doesn't make them great guard dogs, but their tendency to bark at strangers can make them good watchdogs.

"Maltipoos are love wrapped in a cotton-ball cloud of curly fur!" - Unknown

Debunking Maltipoo Myths

Myth 1: Maltipoos Are Not Real Dogs Because They're a Hybrid Breed

This is a common myth not just for Maltipoos but for any mixed breed or "designer" dog. The truth is, all dog breeds we know today came to be through a process of selecting certain traits and breeding for those traits over generations. Maltipoos, like all dogs, are certainly "real" dogs and they offer a unique mix of traits from their parent breeds that many people find desirable.

Myth 2: Maltipoos Are Always Hypoallergenic

While Maltipoos are less likely to cause allergies compared to many other breeds, no dog can be guaranteed 100% hypoallergenic. People allergic to dogs are typically reacting to dander (dead skin cells), saliva, or urine, not just the dog's fur. Maltipoos produce less dander than many breeds, but they do still produce it. If allergies are a concern, spend time with a Maltipoo before bringing one into your home to see how you react.

Myth 3: All Maltipoos Look and Act the Same

Given that Maltipoos are a mix of two different breeds, there's actually quite a bit of variability in their appearance and behavior. As we mentioned earlier, the size and appearance of a Maltipoo can vary greatly depending on the specific traits they inherit from their Maltese and Poodle parents. For instance, some Maltipoos might have a more curly Poodle-like coat, while others might have a straighter, silkier coat like a Maltese. Similarly, while most Maltipoos are friendly and intelligent, their individual personalities can vary, with some being more outgoing and others more reserved.

Myth 4: Maltipoos Are High-strung and Overly Yappy

While it's true that both Maltese and Poodles can be vocal and energetic, it's a misconception that Maltipoos are always high-strung and overly yappy. In fact, many Maltipoos are quite adaptable and can match their energy levels to their environment. Yes, they can be energetic and playful, but they're also known to be great cuddlers who love nothing more than snuggling up with their owners for a cozy nap. As for their yappiness, while Maltipoos might alert bark when someone's at the door, with proper training and socialization, they should not develop problematic barking behaviors.

Myth 5: Maltipoos Don't Need Much Exercise Because They're Small

While it's true that Maltipoos, being small dogs, don't require as much exercise as larger breeds, it's a myth that they hardly need any exercise at all. Like all dogs, Maltipoos need regular physical activity to stay healthy and happy.

These energetic little pups love to play and explore. Regular walks, play sessions, and even dog sports like agility can be a great way to keep your Maltipoo mentally and physically stimulated. So, don't skimp on exercise—your Maltipoo will thank you for it!

> **Tip:** Small dog breeds like Maltipoos can be prone to obesity, so regular exercise, combined with a balanced diet, is crucial to prevent weight-related health issues.

Understanding and debunking these myths are an essential part of being a well-informed Maltipoo owner. By knowing the truth about this breed, you can ensure that a Maltipoo is the right fit for you and that you can provide the right environment for them to thrive.

In the end, Maltipoos are a charming blend of the Poodle and Maltese breeds, offering the best of both worlds. They're intelligent, affectionate, and adorable—making them an increasingly popular choice for individuals and families. As we continue this journey together, you'll discover more about this breed and how to care for a Maltipoo, helping you build a lifelong bond with your furry friend.

CHAPTER 2

Adopting Your Maltipoo
Making an Integral Choice

When it comes to welcoming a new furry family member, especially a Maltipoo, it's a decision that shouldn't be taken lightly. This adorable breed, with its vibrant personality and silky, hypoallergenic coat, will undoubtedly bring joy into your life. However, they also require commitment and care. In this chapter, we will guide you through the process of making an informed choice.

Why Choose a Maltipoo?

Before you embark on your journey of Maltipoo adoption, you might ask: Why choose a Maltipoo? What makes this breed unique?

Maltipoos, as we covered in Chapter 1, are a lovable blend of two purebred parents - the Maltese and the Poodle. These adorable hybrids not only inherit the friendly and intelligent traits of their parents but also come in a manageable size that makes them ideal for various living conditions. Whether you reside in a city apartment or a house with a big backyard, a Maltipoo can adapt and thrive.

> **Fun Fact:** Despite their small size, Maltipoos have a big heart! They're often described as "affection sponges" due to their desire to be near their owners and show love.

Now, let's guide you through the crucial steps of adopting your Maltipoo.

Selecting a Reputable Breeder

If you decide to get your Maltipoo from a breeder, it's crucial to choose a reputable one. Here's a checklist to guide you:

- **Health testing:** A responsible breeder will ensure both parent breeds are tested for common genetic diseases. For Maltipoos, these can include Luxating Patella and Progressive Retinal Atrophy (PRA).

- **Transparent and open:** Reputable breeders are usually more than willing to show you where the puppies and their parents are kept, demonstrating that the dogs are in a safe, clean, and loving environment.

- **Knowledgeable:** A good breeder has extensive knowledge about Maltipoos, including their needs, common health issues, and the traits they inherited from the Maltese and Poodle breeds.

- **References:** Positive references from previous buyers or the local vet can further validate a breeder's reputation.

- **After-sale support:** The breeder should be willing to provide guidance and support after you take your puppy home.

Maltipoos are not officially recognized by major kennel clubs because they are a mixed breed. This makes finding a reputable breeder even more critical!

Considering Adoption

Adoption is another beautiful way to bring a Maltipoo into your life. Animal shelters and rescue groups often have wonderful dogs, including Maltipoos, looking for their forever homes. Here are a few points to consider:

- **Variety:** Rescues have Maltipoos of all ages. While puppies are cute, older dogs can be just as loving and often require less training and attention.

- **Cost:** Adopting from a shelter is typically less expensive than buying from a breeder. The fees often include vaccinations, microchipping, and spaying/neutering, which are additional costs when buying a puppy.

- **Saving a Life:** By adopting, you're providing a home for a dog that may not have had the best start in life.

Remember, rescues and shelters evaluate the dogs in their care for behavior and health issues, so they can help match you with a Maltipoo that fits your lifestyle.

Evaluating Your Maltipoo's Health and Temperament

Whether you're adopting or purchasing your Maltipoo, it's important to evaluate their health and temperament.

- **Health:** A healthy Maltipoo puppy should have clear eyes, clean ears, and a shiny coat. Their environment should be clean, and they should be lively and playful. A health check by a vet is crucial, and a reputable breeder or shelter should provide health certificates for the puppy and their parents.

- **Temperament:** While every Maltipoo has a unique personality, they generally have a friendly disposition. Watch how the puppy interacts with its littermates and how it responds to people. It's a bonus if the puppy is already being socialized to people, other pets, and various environments.

"In the world of dogs, it's not the size of the dog in the fight, it's the size of the fight in the dog." - Mark Twain

Just like Mark Twain said, it's not the size that counts. Even small dogs like Maltipoos have a big spirit and endless love to give.

Assessing Your Lifestyle and Home Environment

Before bringing a Maltipoo home, ensure your lifestyle and environment are suitable. Maltipoos are adaptable but thrive best in certain conditions:

- **Living Space:** Maltipoos, ranging from 8 to 14 inches (20 to 35 cm) in height and weighing around 5 to 20 pounds (2.2 to 9 kg), are perfect for both small apartments and larger homes. However, they need a safe space to play and rest.

- **Time Commitment:** Maltipoos are companion dogs. They crave interaction and don't like to be left alone for long periods. If you're someone with a 9-to-5 job, consider hiring a pet sitter or arranging for a family member to spend time with your Maltipoo during the day.

- **Exercise:** These little bundles of joy are energetic and require daily exercise. Be prepared for walks, playtime, and mental stimulation activities.

- **Other Pets:** Maltipoos typically get along well with other pets, but introductions should be done gradually and under supervision.

Remember, owning a Maltipoo, or any dog, is a long-term commitment. These lovely creatures depend on us for their well-being, and in return, they offer unconditional love and companionship.

Creating a daily schedule for your Maltipoo, including feeding, playtime, training, and rest, can help them adjust faster to their new home.

Adopting a Maltipoo is a significant, life-changing decision, but armed with the right information and mindset, it's one you'll never regret. In the next chapter, we'll delve into how to prepare for the arrival of your new Maltipoo!

CHAPTER 3

Preparing for Your Maltipoo

Creating a Safe and Welcoming Environment

Making the decision to add a Maltipoo to your family is a joyful one, filled with anticipation and excitement. Part of this thrilling journey involves preparing for the arrival of your new furry companion, creating an environment that is not only welcoming but also safe and comforting for them. This chapter will guide you through detailed, practical steps to help you transform your home into a Maltipoo-friendly haven, making your pet's transition as smooth and stress-free as possible.

Comprehensive Guide to Dog-Proofing Your Home

Maltipoos, like other curious creatures, particularly puppies, explore their surroundings with an intriguing blend of excitement and wariness. Therefore, it is vital to make your home a secure place for them by dog-proofing it. This task involves attention to detail and vigilance as you will need to scrutinize every nook and corner of your home. Here is an extensive checklist to help you:

- **Clear The Floor:** Maltipoos are notorious for their inquisitiveness, especially puppies, who will attempt to taste anything they can get their paws on. A crucial first step in dog-proofing your home is to ensure that your floors are free from small, loose items like coins, batteries, and children's toys that could potentially pose a choking hazard. Regularly sweep and vacuum your floors to prevent any unwanted incidents.

- **Protect Power Cords:** The dangling nature of power cords can make them an irresistible chew toy for a Maltipoo. Consider investing in cord protectors or rearrange your furniture, so cords are hidden or inaccessible. This prevents electrocution or any damage to your electronic devices.

- **Secure Cabinets:** Many household items that are safe for humans can be toxic or harmful to your Maltipoo. Install safety locks, similar to baby locks, on lower cabinets, particularly those containing cleaning supplies, medications, or food items. Keeping these substances out of their reach is crucial to their safety.

- **Control Access:** Certain areas of your home might not be safe for your Maltipoo, especially if you have stairs or rooms with delicate items. Using baby gates to restrict access to these areas can be particularly helpful in maintaining your Maltipoo's safety and preserving the order in your home.

- **Trash Bins:** A trash bin can seem like a treasure chest to a curious Maltipoo. Make sure all trash bins have a secure lid or are tucked away in a closet or under the sink. Trash can contain harmful items like spoiled food, sharp objects, or small items that can be a choking hazard.

- **Plants:** While adding a touch of nature to your home, many common household plants can be toxic to dogs. Research or consult a plant expert to ensure all plants in your home are safe for pets, or keep them out of your Maltipoo's reach.

Did you know that some common houseplants like lilies, azaleas, and sago palms are toxic to dogs? It's crucial to verify if a plant is pet-safe before bringing it into your home.

Creating a Luxuriously Comfortable Space

Just like humans, your Maltipoo will appreciate having a personal space—a safe haven they can retreat to when they need rest or feel overwhelmed. This space could be a cozy crate, a plush dog bed, or a dedicated corner of a room furnished with comforts. Here's how to make their space as comfortable as possible:

- **Crates:** Crates can offer a sense of security to your Maltipoo. If you decide to crate train your Maltipoo, select a crate that's large enough for them to stand, turn around, and lie down comfortably. It should offer enough room for their comfort but not be so large that they might designate a corner for elimination, which can hinder house training. For a full-grown Maltipoo, a crate that's approximately 24 inches (60 cm) in length should suffice.

- **Beds:** Alternatively, you could choose a dog bed instead of a crate for your Maltipoo's personal space. It should be snug, comfortable, and easy to clean. Beds with raised sides, often known as cuddler beds, can offer a sense of security and warmth. Consider the material and filling of the bed to ensure it provides adequate support and comfort.

- **Blankets and Toys:** Adding soft blankets and a selection of chew toys can add extra comfort to their space. Toys can also serve as a means of entertainment when they are in their space.

Consider adding an item that carries your scent, like an old t-shirt, to their sleeping area. Your scent can provide a sense of comfort and familiarity, which can aid in their adjustment and bonding process with you.

Comprehensive List of Essential Supplies

To ensure your Maltipoo's well-being and happiness, you will need to stock up on a variety of supplies ranging from feeding to grooming. Here is an exhaustive list of the essentials:

1. **Food and Water Bowls:** Choose sturdy and durable bowls for feeding and hydrating your Maltipoo. Ceramic or stainless-steel bowls are great options—they are robust, easy to clean, and do not harbor bacteria like plastic ones. Maltipoos are small dogs, so shallow, wide bowls would be perfect.

2. **Food:** Proper nutrition is vital to your Maltipoo's

growth, health, and well-being. Consult with your vet or breeder about the best puppy food for your new pet. Keep in mind that as your Maltipoo grows, their dietary needs will evolve, requiring a transition to adult dog food.

3. **Collar and Leash:** Your Maltipoo will need a lightweight, adjustable collar that can grow with them and a light leash that's easy for them to get used to. Reflective or light-up options can be useful for evening walks.

4. **ID Tag:** An ID tag is an essential accessory for your Maltipoo's collar. The tag should have your contact information—an extra layer of security if they ever get lost.

5. **Toys:** To keep your Maltipoo entertained and mentally stimulated, provide a variety of toys. Chew toys, soft toys, squeaky toys, and puzzle toys that challenge their brain are all great choices.

6. **Grooming Supplies:** Regular grooming is necessary to keep your Maltipoo looking their best. Grooming essentials include a soft-bristle brush, dog-friendly shampoo, a toothbrush and toothpaste suitable for dogs, and nail clippers. Maltipoos have hair, not fur, so their grooming needs are a bit more specif-

ic—much like our own!

Did You Know? Unlike dogs with fur, Maltipoos' hair continues to grow, much like human hair. This means they don't shed as much, but they require regular grooming sessions and haircuts!

Introducing Your Maltipoo to Their New Home

After the process of dog-proofing your home and creating a cozy, personal space for your Maltipoo, it's finally time to introduce your furry friend to their new environment. This can be an overwhelming experience for your puppy, so take it slow and steady. Introduce them to their designated area first and gradually allow them to explore the rest of the house at their own pace. Patience is key during this process—your Maltipoo may take several days or even weeks to adjust fully to their new surroundings.

> "Patience and perseverance have a magical effect before which difficulties disappear and obstacles vanish." – John Quincy Adams

In conclusion, preparing your home for your new Maltipoo is a meticulous process that involves creating a safe, welcoming environment, gathering necessary supplies, and gently introducing your home to them. Each Maltipoo has a unique personality, and as you get to know yours, you may need to tweak your preparations to suit their individual preferences and behaviors. All these efforts will undoubtedly pay off as you watch your Maltipoo comfortably settle into their new home, infusing it with warmth and love, and filling your life with joy, companionship, and wonderful memories.

CHAPTER 4

Settling Your Maltipoo
Managing the First Few Days and Nights

The first few days and nights with your new Maltipoo will be a mix of joy, excitement, and, quite naturally, a little uncertainty—both for you and your pup. Understanding how to manage this crucial transition period can significantly impact your Maltipoo's ease of adjustment and their bond with you. This chapter aims to provide clear and practical guidelines to help you establish routines, introduce your pup to their new environment, and set ground rules—all with the warmth, patience, and love your Maltipoo needs during this time.

The Importance of Routine

Dogs are creatures of habit, and the Maltipoo is no exception. Establishing a consistent routine right from the start will provide a sense of security for your pup and help them understand what to expect from their daily life.

- **Feeding Routine:** Maltipoo puppies generally need to eat three to four times a day. Choose specific times for each meal and stick to them. An example schedule could be 7 AM, 12 PM, and 5 PM. Adjust the times to fit your schedule, but remember to keep them consistent.

- **Exercise and Play Time:** Like all puppies, Maltipoos have a lot of energy and need regular play and exercise. Schedule several short play sessions throughout the day. For example, a short walk in the morning, mid-day playtime, an evening walk, and a quick play session before bed can work well.

- **Potty Breaks:** Young puppies need frequent potty breaks. Generally, you should take them outside every 2-3 hours and always after meals, playtimes, and naps. At night, aim for at least one midnight break until they can hold it for longer.

Did you know a puppy can control their bladder one hour for every month of age? So, a three-month-old Maltipoo puppy can hold it in for about three hours.

- **Quiet Time and Sleep:** Maltipoos, especially puppies, need a lot of sleep—around 14-18 hours per day. Schedule quiet times during the day and establish a consistent bedtime.

Pro Tip: Use both verbal and visual cues to signal different parts of your Maltipoo's routine. For instance, saying "bedtime" each night before guiding them to their bed helps reinforce the routine.

Introducing Your Maltipoo to New Environments

As your Maltipoo acclimates to their new home, it's essential to gradually expose them to a variety of environments and stimuli. This process, known as socialization, is crucial for their development and comfort with new experiences.

1. **Inside the Home:** Allow your Maltipoo to explore different rooms under your supervision. Introduce them to various sounds such as the vacuum cleaner, washing machine, or doorbell.

2. **Outside the Home:** Once they've settled inside, introduce your Maltipoo to the backyard, then the front yard, and finally, the neighborhood. Always ensure they're safe and secure on a leash.

3. **Meeting New People and Animals:** Introduce your

Maltipoo to different people—men, women, children—and other animals. Remember to keep these interactions positive and supervised.

4. **Experiencing Different Situations:** Expose your Maltipoo to different experiences like car rides, walks in the park, and visits to the vet. The goal is to help them become a well-adjusted, confident adult dog.

Socialization should be a positive experience for your Maltipoo. Never force your puppy into a situation

that frightens them. Instead, gently encourage them and reward them for their bravery.

Establishing House Rules and Managing Separation Anxiety

Setting clear rules from the start is crucial. Decide where your Maltipoo is allowed to go, when and where they will eat, sleep, and play. Consistency is key—ensure all family members understand and follow the same rules.

While your Maltipoo adjusts to their new home, they might experience separation anxiety when left alone. To manage this, start by leaving your Maltipoo alone for short periods, gradually increasing the duration. Providing a comforting toy or a piece of clothing that smells like you can also help them feel more secure.

> "In life, change is inevitable. In business, change is vital." - Warren G. Bennis. The same goes for the life of a young Maltipoo navigating the changes in their new environment!

Dealing with the First Nights

The first nights with your Maltipoo might be challenging. Your puppy may cry or whine due to the sudden separation from their littermates. Patience and understanding are key during this time.

- **Bedtime Routine:** Establish a calming bedtime routine. This could include a final potty break, some gentle play or cuddling, and then settling them into their bed with a soft word of goodnight.

- **Nighttime Cries:** If your Maltipoo cries at night, resist the urge to rush to them immediately. If they learn that crying gets your attention, it could reinforce the behavior. Instead, wait for a break in the crying to check on them. If they're safe and don't need a potty break, gently reassure them and then leave—your consistent response will help them learn to self-soothe.

- **Midnight Potty Breaks:** Remember, young puppies can't hold their bladder all night. Set an alarm for a midnight potty break. Over time, as your Maltipoo grows, they'll be able to hold it in longer, and this break will no longer be necessary.

A puppy's crying can tug at your heartstrings, but remember, "Patience is bitter, but its fruit is sweet." - Jean-Jacques Rousseau. Your understanding during these first few nights will pay off as your Maltipoo adjusts and starts sleeping peacefully through the night.

By providing routine, gradually introducing new environments, establishing house rules, and managing the initial nights with understanding, you're building a strong foundation for your relationship with your Maltipoo. In this phase, as you're teaching them about their new world, remember also to learn from them—about their unique personality, their communication style, and the boundless love they have to offer. After all, the joy of bringing a Maltipoo into your home is not just in teaching, but also in learning and growing together.

> *"Everyone thinks they have the best dog. And none of them are wrong." - W.R. Purche*

Your journey with your Maltipoo is unique and special, and every day brings new opportunities for joy, love, and shared experiences.

CHAPTER 5

Maltipoo Puppy Essentials

Socialization, Training, and Early Care

Having successfully navigated the first few days and nights with your Maltipoo puppy, you're now entering an exciting and crucial phase of their development. This chapter will explore the importance of socialization, offer a guide to basic puppy training, and provide guidance on the early care of your Maltipoo puppy.

The Significance of Early Socialization

Socialization plays a pivotal role in the development of your Maltipoo puppy. As Aristotle once wisely stated, "Give me a child until he is 7 and I will show you the man." While this famous quote was intended for humans, it serves as a compelling metaphor for the critical early stages of your Maltipoo's life. By exposing your Maltipoo to a range of people, environments, and experiences during their formative weeks, you are laying the foundation for a confident, well-adjusted adult dog.

Without proper socialization, your Maltipoo may become overly fearful or even aggressive when encountering new experiences, which can result in significant behavior problems down the line.

When to Start Socialization?

The optimal window for socializing your Maltipoo puppy falls between 3 and 16 weeks of age. During this stage, puppies are naturally more open and receptive to new experiences. This is the perfect opportunity to introduce them to a wide range of sights, sounds, smells, people, and animals.

How to Socialize Your Maltipoo Puppy?

1. **Expose them to different environments:** Start by allowing your puppy to explore your home in its entirety. From the living room to the laundry room, each space offers unique sounds, smells, and experiences. Gradually take them on outings to places like parks, pet stores, and quieter city streets. Remember to keep your puppy safe from potential disease risks by avoiding areas frequented by unvaccinated dogs until your vet gives you the green light.

2. **Introduce them to various people:** Maltipoos are naturally social dogs, so meeting a variety of people

should be a positive experience for them. Make sure they meet individuals of all ages, from children to seniors, and people wearing various types of clothing—hats, sunglasses, uniforms—to help your puppy feel comfortable with anyone they might meet in the future.

3. **Familiarize them with other animals:** Start introducing your Maltipoo to other friendly, vaccinated dogs. Organize playdates or take them to a puppy socialization class. Meeting other types of animals, like cats or rabbits, can also help broaden their experiences.

4. **Acclimate them to different sounds and situations:** The world is full of strange and potentially startling sounds. From the noise of household appliances to traffic noises and thunderstorms, helping your puppy get used to a wide range of sounds can prevent sound phobias later in life.

The 'fear imprint period' of puppies, which occurs between 8 and 10 weeks of age, is a critical time during which traumatic experiences can have lasting impacts. During this time, ensure all experiences are positive.

Training Your Maltipoo Puppy: Building the Foundations of Good Behavior

Just as we provide education for our children, early training is crucial for your Maltipoo puppy. Training offers a framework of rules and expectations that guide their behavior, helping to prevent problems before they develop.

- **Toilet Training:** This is typically the first challenge for new puppy owners. Establishing a consistent routine is key to successful house training. Feed your puppy at the same times each day, and take them out to their bathroom spot every 2 hours, as well as after meals and naps. Always take them to the same spot and use a keyword such as "potty," rewarding them lavishly when they do their business. It's important to remember that accidents will happen—puppy bladders don't have the same control as adult dogs. Patience and consistency are key.

- **Bite Inhibition:** Teething and learning to control the strength of their bite is a normal part of puppy development. Instead of punishing them for biting, provide appropriate chew toys, and encourage play-biting with these toys instead of your hands or feet.

- **Basic Commands:** Training your Maltipoo to respond to basic commands such as "Sit," "Stay," "Come," and "Leave it," is a critical part of their early education. Keep training sessions short and fun, with plenty of rewards for success.

Providing Essential Early Care for Your Maltipoo Puppy

The early care you provide for your Maltipoo puppy not only impacts their immediate health and wellbeing but sets the stage for their health in adulthood.

- **Balanced Diet:** Just like human babies, puppies have different nutritional needs than adults. Puppies are growing rapidly, and their diet should support that growth. Look for a high-quality puppy food that is rich in proteins and fats from reliable sources, along with a balanced ratio of calcium and phosphorus to support bone development.

- **Adequate Exercise:** Exercise is essential for a happy, healthy Maltipoo puppy. However, over-exercising your Maltipoo during puppyhood can result in joint and bone problems. Aim for several short periods of exercise each day, rather than one or two long walks or play sessions.

- **Regular Vet Check-ups:** Your vet is your partner in ensuring your Maltipoo puppy grows up healthy. Regular vet check-ups, staying on schedule with vaccinations, and regular deworming and flea and tick prevention are all essential aspects of puppy care.

In the immortal words of Benjamin Franklin, "An ounce of prevention is worth a pound of cure." By providing the right early care for your Maltipoo, you're setting them up for a lifetime of good health.

To conclude, the early months of your Maltipoo's life are an exciting journey filled with critical developmental milestones. As their companion and caretaker, your role in guiding them through this period is invaluable. Through careful socialization, you're helping them become confident and adaptable. By laying the groundwork for their training, you're setting clear expectations for their behavior. Lastly, with proper early care, you're giving them the best possible start to a long, healthy life. Every step of this journey is an opportunity to deepen your bond and understanding of your Maltipoo, shaping them into the delightful, loving companion they're meant to be.

CHAPTER 6

Maltipoo Training Fundamentals

Positive Reinforcement and Essential Commands

Learning is a crucial part of any puppy's life, and it is even more vital for a hybrid breed like the Maltipoo. Training your Maltipoo puppy can be an enjoyable and fulfilling experience. Armed with patience, consistency, and a pocket full of treats, you're ready to embark on this training journey. This chapter will take you through the principles of positive reinforcement training, how to teach essential commands, and provide insights into leash and grooming training.

The Power of Positive Reinforcement

Positive reinforcement is a method that uses rewards to encourage the repeat of a particular behavior. In dog training, this means rewarding your Maltipoo for performing the behavior you're trying to teach.

Steps to Implement Positive Reinforcement

1. **Choose the Reward:** Every Maltipoo is unique, so the reward that works best can vary. It could be a small treat, a favorite toy, or even simple praise. It's important to find something that your Maltipoo genuinely loves and responds to.

2. **Cue the Behavior:** Once you've chosen the reward, you'll need to cue the behavior. This could be a verbal command, like "sit," or a hand signal.

3. **Reward Promptly:** The moment your Maltipoo performs the desired behavior, you should immediately give them the reward. Timing is key—don't delay the reward, or your pup might not connect it with their action.

4. **Practice Consistently:** Consistency is vital for successful training. Keep repeating the behavior-reward process until your Maltipoo understands and performs the behavior consistently.

Teaching Essential Commands

Now that you're familiar with the positive reinforcement method, let's look at how to apply it to teaching essential commands. Each command is a step-by-step process that requires patience and consistency.

"Sit" Command

The "Sit" command is often the first command owners teach. It is a fundamental behavior that can help in various situations and is relatively easy for your Maltipoo to learn.

1. **Get your Maltipoo's attention** by holding a treat near their nose, but don't let them grab it right away.

2. **Lift your hand slowly** and allow your Maltipoo's head to follow the treat. As their gaze follows the upward movement, their bottom should naturally move into a sitting position.

3. The moment their bottom touches the floor, say **"Sit"** in a clear, happy tone.

4. **Immediately give them the treat and plenty of praise.** This positive reinforcement will make them want to repeat the action.

Repeat these steps several times each training session. It won't be long before your Maltipoo associates the word "Sit" with the action and the reward.

"Stay" Command

The "Stay" command is crucial for your Maltipoo's safety, helping to keep them in one place despite distractions.

1. Start by asking your Maltipoo to "Sit."

2. Open your palm towards your dog like a stop sign, and say "Stay" in a clear, calm voice.

3. Slowly take a step back. If your Maltipoo stays put, immediately reward them with a treat and praise.

4. Repeat the exercise, gradually increasing the distance between you and your Maltipoo. Remember to reward them each time they successfully stay.

Patience is key with the "Stay" command. It can take several training sessions for your Maltipoo to fully grasp the concept.

"Come" Command

The "Come" command is essential for getting your Maltipoo to return to you on command, a crucial skill for their safety.

1. Put a collar and leash on your Maltipoo. Stand a few feet away.

2. Bend down to your Maltipoo's level and say "Come" in a clear, excited tone. You can also pat your thighs to encourage them towards you.

3. When your Maltipoo comes to you, reward them with a treat and praise. Make sure this experience is overwhelmingly positive.

Repeat this command in different environments with various distractions to ensure your Maltipoo will always come when called.

"Leave It" Command

The "Leave It" command helps keep your Maltipoo safe by preventing them from picking up dangerous items.

1. Hold a treat in both hands. Show your Maltipoo one treat and then close your fist around it. Say "Leave it."

2. Your Maltipoo will likely try to get the treat, sniffing, licking, and pawing at your hand. Ignore these behaviors.

3. When your Maltipoo stops trying and moves away, say "Good leave it!" Then, give them the treat from your other hand.

4. Repeat this until your Maltipoo moves away from the first treat when you give the command.

Remember, the "Leave It" command can take time to master, so be patient and consistent in your training.

Training commands to your Maltipoo might seem daunting at first, but with consistency and a positive attitude, your furry friend will soon be impressing you with their obedience. Make sure to keep each training session fun and stress-free. As famed animal behaviorist, Ian Dunbar, said, "Training dogs to like, love and look forward to their training sessions should be your primary focus, everything else will fall into place provided you are kind and gentle and lavish with your praise and rewards."

Be patient and consistent in your training. Some Maltipoos might pick up commands faster than others. It's essential not to compare your pup's progress with others and instead focus on their individual learning pace.

Leash Training Your Maltipoo

Leash training is crucial for Maltipoos as it ensures their safety and keeps them under control during walks. It can start as soon as they've settled into their new home.

- **Introduce the Leash and Collar:** Let your Maltipoo sniff and explore their new leash and collar. Gradually have them wear it for short periods.

- **Start Indoors:** Begin the training indoors, where there are fewer distractions. Allow them to drag the leash around to get used to its weight.

- **Practice Walking:** Encourage your Maltipoo to walk by calling their name or using a treat. Reward them for following you.

- **Gradual Outdoor Exposure:** Once comfortable indoors, take your Maltipoo outside. Start in your backyard or a quiet area to minimize distractions.

- **Be Consistent:** If your Maltipoo pulls on the leash, stop walking. This teaches them that pulling won't get them anywhere.

Grooming Training: A Maltipoo's Journey to Comfortable Grooming

Given their Poodle heritage, Maltipoos often have curly or wavy fur that requires regular grooming. Here's how to make grooming a positive experience:

1. **Gradual Exposure:** Introduce grooming tools one at a time. Let your Maltipoo sniff and investigate them.

2. **Reward Compliance:** If your Maltipoo lets you

brush a few strokes or clip one nail, reward them immediately.

3. **Create a Routine:** Consistent grooming at the same time and place helps your Maltipoo understand what to expect.

4. **Keep it Positive:** Speak in a soothing tone and give lots of praise during grooming sessions.

In conclusion, training your Maltipoo is a continual process that strengthens your bond and ensures their safety. By using positive reinforcement and gradual exposure, you can help your Maltipoo become a well-behaved and happy companion.

As dog trainer and television personality Victoria Stilwell said, "Training is not a luxury, but a key component to good animal care." Everyone loves a well-trained dog—they're safer, happier, and make life easier and more fun for their owners. But remember, the journey of training is equally important as the destination. Enjoy the process and the precious moments of growth it brings.

CHAPTER 7

Maltipoo Nutrition
Ensuring a Balanced Diet

A healthy Maltipoo is a happy Maltipoo, and nutrition is an essential component of your furry friend's overall health. With a correctly balanced diet, your Maltipoo can maintain an ideal weight, a healthy coat, and an energetic lifestyle.

The word 'Maltipoo' is a portmanteau of Maltese and Poodle, just like 'brunch' is a blend of breakfast and lunch!

Choosing the Right Food for Your Maltipoo

Every dog has unique nutritional needs, and the Maltipoo is no exception. Factors such as your dog's age, size, activity level, and overall health will dictate the type and amount of food they require.

Dry Kibble vs. Wet Food: The Age-Old Debate

One of the first decisions you'll need to make when feeding your Maltipoo is choosing between dry and wet food. Each has its benefits:

- **Dry Kibble:** Kibble is often more economical and easier to store. It's also beneficial for dental health, as the act of chewing can help scrape plaque off your Maltipoo's teeth.

- **Wet Food:** This type of food is generally more palatable to dogs and can be a good option for picky eaters. It also helps with hydration.

Many Maltipoo owners opt for a combination of both wet and dry food. This allows you to take advantage of the benefits of both types while providing a varied and exciting diet for your pet.

Commercial vs. Homemade Diets

Choosing between commercial and homemade diets is another important decision.

- **Commercial Diets:** High-quality commercial dog foods are carefully formulated to provide a balanced diet for your Maltipoo. They're convenient and come in a wide range of formulas targeted at specific life stages, breed sizes, and health needs.

- **Homemade Diets:** Homemade diets allow you to have complete control over what your Maltipoo eats. However, it's crucial to work with a pet nutrition expert or veterinarian to ensure that your homemade diet meets all your Maltipoo's nutritional needs.

Tip: If you're feeding your Maltipoo a homemade diet, consider making homemade treats as well! They can be a healthy and tasty supplement to their meals.

Understanding Nutrient Needs

A balanced diet for your Maltipoo should contain the right mix of proteins, fats, carbohydrates, vitamins, and minerals.

Proteins

Proteins are essential for growth, maintenance, and repair of body tissues. They also play a role in the creation of antibodies, which help combat infections. As a general rule, a healthy adult Maltipoo's diet should be approximately 18% protein, while puppies and lactating females require around 22%.

Choose high-quality, easily digestible animal proteins like chicken, turkey, fish, or lamb. Avoid foods with vague descriptions like "meat by-products," which can include low-quality protein sources.

Fats

Fats provide the most concentrated source of energy for your Maltipoo. They are essential for absorbing vitamins and protecting nerves. Additionally, fats contribute to skin and coat health. Aim for a diet with approximately 5% fat for adult Maltipoos, while puppies and lactating females should have around 8%.

Good sources of fats include named animal fats (like chicken fat) and fish oils, which are high in Omega-3 fatty acids.

Carbohydrates

Carbohydrates provide your Maltipoo with energy and are important for gastrointestinal health. Look for dog food with high-quality, digestible carbohydrates like whole grains or vegetables. Avoid foods with added sugars.

Vitamins and Minerals

Vitamins and minerals are crucial for various metabolic functions. They're usually provided in adequate amounts in a balanced commercial diet, but if you're preparing a homemade diet, you might need to add a multivitamin supplement.

Consult with your vet or a pet nutritionist to make sure your homemade diet is balanced and complete.

Common Food Allergies and Intolerances in Maltipoos

Like their parent breeds, Maltipoos can be prone to food allergies or intolerances. The most common allergens include beef, dairy, wheat, egg, chicken, lamb, soy, pork, rabbit, and fish.

If your Maltipoo is experiencing symptoms like itching, redness, chronic ear infections, gastrointestinal upset, or poor coat quality, they could be reacting to something in their diet. Consult with your vet for diagnosis and advice on dietary changes.

Remember: Always introduce new foods gradually to monitor for any adverse reactions.

Maintaining a Healthy Weight

Keeping your Maltipoo at a healthy weight is crucial for their overall health. Obesity can lead to numerous health issues, including heart disease, diabetes, and joint problems.

Adult Maltipoos typically weigh between 5-20 pounds (2.2-9 kilograms). Their ideal weight will depend on factors like their gender, age, and individual physique. Your vet can help determine your Maltipoo's ideal weight.

Regular exercise and portion control are key in maintaining a healthy weight. Feed your Maltipoo measured amounts at scheduled times rather than leaving food out all day. Treats should make up no more than 10% of your Maltipoo's daily caloric intake.

Remember, the feeding guidelines on pet food packages are just that - guidelines. Every Maltipoo is unique, and their caloric needs will vary. Work with your vet to determine the right amount of food for your pet.

To quote Ann Wigmore, a holistic health practitioner, "The food you eat can be either the safest and most powerful form of medicine or the slowest form of poison." With the right diet, you can ensure your Maltipoo thrives, living a long, happy, and healthy life by your side.

CHAPTER 8

Exercise and Enrichment for Your Maltipoo

"Maltipoos are the embodiment of joy wrapped in fur. Their sheer energy and excitement for life are contagious. As an owner, it's your job to ensure this energy has a healthy outlet," as remarked by renowned dog behaviorist, Cesar Millan. This chapter will delve into the unique exercise needs of your Maltipoo, provide ideas for mental stimulation, and guide you to recognize signs of over-exertion.

Maltipoos, like their Poodle parents, have a surprising amount of energy for their small size!

The Maltipoo Exercise Equation

All dogs require physical exercise to maintain a healthy body and mind, but the type, intensity, and duration of the activity can vary widely among breeds. As a hybrid of the Maltese and Poodle, the Maltipoo embodies a perfect mix of vigor and adaptability, demanding an exercise regime that matches its energetic yet companionable nature.

Activity Level and Duration

Adult Maltipoos are energetic and require a moderate level of exercise to keep them healthy and happy. On average, a Maltipoo should get at least 30 to 60 minutes of exercise each day. This could include walks, playtime, or training activities. Puppies may require shorter, more frequent bouts of exercise.

Regular exercise helps manage weight, enhances muscle tone, promotes good digestion, and is essential for overall physical health. Additionally, it helps prevent behavior issues that could arise from boredom or pent-up energy.

Remember, Maltipoos love companionship! They'll be happiest if their exercise routine involves quality time with their favorite human - you.

Types of Physical Exercise

When it comes to physical exercise, variety is key to keep your Maltipoo interested and engaged. Here are some favorites:

- **Walks:** A daily walk or two is essential. Try different routes to give your Maltipoo new sceneries and smells to explore.

- **Playtime:** Fetch, tug-of-war, or simply running around in a safe, fenced area are great ways to burn energy. Maltipoos love their toys, so keep a variety on hand.

- **Training:** Obedience training, tricks, or even agility (for older dogs) can provide both physical and mental exercise.

- **Doggy Playdates:** If your Maltipoo is social, occasional playdates with other small dogs can be a fun way to burn off energy and socialize.

Pro tip: Try using a puzzle toy during playtime to provide both mental and physical stimulation!

Mental Stimulation for a Sharp Maltipoo Mind

As descendants of the intelligent Poodle, Maltipoos thrive on mental stimulation. Keeping their minds active reduces boredom, which can lead to destructive behaviors, and helps keep them mentally sharp.

Puzzle Toys

Puzzle toys are fantastic tools for mental stimulation. They come in various difficulties, making them great for all life stages. These toys usually involve hiding treats inside, which your Maltipoo then has to figure out how to access. It's like a game and a reward all in one!

Training Sessions

Training sessions are not just for teaching your Maltipoo manners and tricks. They're also a great way to challenge their minds. Regular short training sessions using positive reinforcement techniques can be a fun and rewarding mental workout.

Interactive Games

Games that require your Maltipoo to think can be very stimulating. These could be as simple as hiding a treat or a favorite toy and encouraging your Maltipoo to find it.

Rotate Toys

To keep things fresh, try rotating your Maltipoo's toys every week. This way, every time a toy comes out of the rotation, it'll feel like a brand new toy to your Maltipoo.

Remember, a tired dog is a good dog. A Maltipoo that's had its fill of physical and mental exercise is more likely to be calm at home.

Signs of Over-exertion and Adjusting Exercise

Even though Maltipoos are energetic, it's crucial to avoid over-exertion. Over-exertion can lead to exhaustion, heatstroke, or even injury. Signs of over-exertion include heavy panting, drooling, confusion, weakness, vomiting, or diarrhea. In extreme cases, your Maltipoo may collapse.

If you see any signs of over-exertion, stop the exercise immediately, offer your Maltipoo water, and let them rest in a cool, shaded area. If they don't recover quickly, contact your vet immediately.

Adjust the exercise routine if necessary. You might need to shorten the duration or decrease the intensity, especially during hot weather. Always remember to bring water for both you and your Maltipoo during outdoor activities.

When it comes to exercising your Maltipoo, the key is to find a balance between keeping them physically active and mentally stimulated without overdoing it. Your Maltipoo's exercise needs will change as they grow and age, so staying attuned to their needs and adjusting their activities accordingly will help keep them at their happiest and healthiest.

As the saying goes, "A tired Maltipoo is a happy Maltipoo". With the right balance of physical exercise, mental stimulation, and rest, your Maltipoo will lead a fulfilling and joyous life. Enjoy the journey!

CHAPTER 9

Maltipoo Health and Wellness
Regular Check-Ups and Preventative Care

"Until one has loved an animal, a part of one's soul remains unawakened," as famously remarked by French writer Anatole France. But love is not just about cuddles and playtime; it also involves safeguarding your furry friend's health. Welcome to Chapter 9, where we delve into the world of Maltipoo health and wellness, covering everything from common health issues and preventative care to oral hygiene and the role of genetic testing.

The Need for Regular Vet Visits

Maltipoos, like all dogs, benefit significantly from regular veterinary check-ups. An annual vet visit helps keep track of your Maltipoo's health and catch any potential issues early.

Your vet will examine your Maltipoo from head to tail, assessing body condition, listening to the heart and lungs, checking eyes, ears, and teeth, and feeling the abdomen and joints. They'll also ask about your Maltipoo's behavior, diet, and exercise.

Vet visits are also the time for essential vaccinations, parasite prevention, and health screenings. Remember, an ounce of prevention is worth a pound of cure!

Maltipoo-Specific Health Issues

Although Maltipoos are generally healthy dogs, they're prone to certain health conditions inherited from their Maltese and Poodle parents. Understanding these potential issues helps you spot signs early and seek timely treatment.

Patellar Luxation

This condition, also known as "slipped stifles," is common in small dogs. It happens when the patella, which has three parts — the femur (thigh bone), patella (knee cap), and tibia (calf) — is not properly lined up. This misalignment can cause limping or an abnormal gait, almost like a skip or a hop.

Progressive Retinal Atrophy (PRA)

This is a degenerative eye disorder that eventually leads to blindness. PRA is detectable years before your Maltipoo becomes blind, emphasizing the need for regular vet visits.

Thankfully, dogs adapt well to blindness with their keen senses of smell and hearing.

White Shaker Syndrome

This condition, seen more often in small, white dogs, causes a range of neurological issues, including tremors, unsteady gait, and rapid eye movements. It's not fully understood but is believed to be an autoimmune disorder. Treatment usually involves steroids and improves the condition significantly.

Epilepsy

Epilepsy causes seizures in dogs, which can be scary to witness. If your Maltipoo is diagnosed with epilepsy, your vet can prescribe medication to manage the condition.

Keeping Maltipoo's Ears Clean

Maltipoos inherit their parent Poodle's floppy ears, which can be prone to infections because of less air circulation. To prevent this, you should regularly check your Maltipoo's ears and clean them as needed.

1. **Checking the Ears:** Healthy dog ears should be clean and pink with a slight yeasty smell. If you notice redness, swelling, a strong odor, or discharge, these could be signs of an infection, and it's time to consult your vet.

2. **Cleaning the Ears:** Use a vet-approved canine ear cleaner. Don't use water or vinegar, as these can lead to irritation or infections.

- Saturate a cotton ball or pad with the ear cleaner.

- Gently wipe the inside of the ear flap and around the outer ear canal opening.

- Be careful not to go too deep into the ear canal, as you could cause injury.

- If your Maltipoo seems to be uncomfortable, stop and consult with your vet.

Remember, over-cleaning can also cause issues by disrupting the natural balance in your Maltipoo's ears. Stick to cleaning when necessary, or as advised by your vet.

Maltipoo Oral Hygiene: More than Fresh Breath

Oral hygiene is vital for your Maltipoo's overall health. Poor dental hygiene can lead to dental diseases that could cause tooth loss and can even impact the heart and kidneys.

Regular brushing (daily is ideal but aim for at least three times a week) and dental chews can help maintain oral health. Your vet should also do a dental health check during annual visits and may recommend a professional dental clean under anesthesia if necessary.

Dental Hygiene: How to Clean Your Maltipoo's Teeth

Regular tooth brushing is an essential part of your Maltipoo's oral hygiene. Here's a step-by-step guide:

- **Choose the Right Tools:** Use a dog toothbrush or finger brush and a canine toothpaste. Never use human toothpaste as it contains ingredients that are harmful to dogs if swallowed.

- **Get Your Maltipoo Used to the Idea:** Start by letting your Maltipoo taste the toothpaste. Then, try touching their mouth and teeth with your finger. Gradually work up to a toothbrush. This process may take a few days.

- **Brushing:** Apply a small amount of toothpaste to the toothbrush. Lift your Maltipoo's upper lip and start brushing in a circular motion, focusing on the gum line. Remember to get the back upper molars and canines, as these areas are prone to tartar buildup. Ideally, aim for two minutes per session.

- **Post-Brushing:** Reward your Maltipoo with praise and a dental chew. There's no need to rinse their mouth, as dog toothpaste is meant to be swallowed.

- **Frequency:** Aim to brush your Maltipoo's teeth daily. If this isn't feasible, aim for at least three times per week.

Remember, dental care isn't just about fresh breath; it can significantly impact your Maltipoo's overall health. Regular brushing and professional cleanings as needed will help keep your Maltipoo's mouth healthy.

Genetic Testing: Knowledge is Power

Genetic testing for dogs has become increasingly popular, and it's easy to see why. These tests can reveal breed ancestry, but importantly, they can also screen for various genetic diseases, including those common in Maltipoos.

If you're getting a Maltipoo puppy, a reputable breeder should provide genetic testing results for the parent dogs. But if that's not available or you're curious about your adopted Maltipoo's health, you can pursue testing with your vet's guidance.

As the saying goes, "Forewarned is forearmed." Knowing your Maltipoo's genetic predispositions allows you to be vigilant about related symptoms and, in some cases, take preventive steps.

Contrary to what you might think, a dog's mouth isn't cleaner than a human's! Dogs have as many bacteria in their mouths as we do. However, their bacteria are different from ours, which is why dog bites can lead to infections. Regular oral hygiene for your Maltipoo is crucial.

Healthcare may not be the most fun aspect of owning a Maltipoo, but it's undoubtedly one of the most important. Regular vet visits, understanding common health issues, maintaining good oral hygiene, and considering genetic testing's valuable insights are all key to ensuring your Maltipoo lives a long, happy, and healthy life. After all, as British poet Lord Byron inscribed on his dog's tomb, "His beauty, his courage, his swift pace... but his love, his love was above all."

CHAPTER 10

Traveling with Your Maltipoo
Ensuring Safe and Enjoyable Journeys

Traveling with your Maltipoo can be a delightful experience if planned well. These adaptable and friendly pups often enjoy exploring new environments, meeting new people and, of course, spending more quality time with you. This chapter will help you navigate the logistics of traveling with your Maltipoo and ensure that you and your furry friend can enjoy every journey together safely and happily.

Planning Ahead for the Trip

Travel Essentials for Your Maltipoo

Pack your Maltipoo's travel kit to ensure your fur baby has all the essentials. Here are some items that should make it into your Maltipoo's travel bag:

- **Food and Water:** Don't forget to pack enough of your Maltipoo's regular food for the duration of your trip, plus a little extra. Changing their diet suddenly can lead to digestive issues, and it might be challenging to find the exact brand or type of food they're accustomed to while traveling. Portable water bottles with attached bowls or collapsible travel bowls are ideal for providing water on the go.

- **Leash and Harness:** It's important to keep your Maltipoo secured when in unfamiliar territory. A well-fitted harness and leash are crucial for controlling your Maltipoo in crowded or unfamiliar places.

- **Toys and Chews:** Familiar toys and chews can provide comfort and entertainment for your Maltipoo during travel.

- **Blankets and Bedding:** A familiar blanket or portable bed can help your Maltipoo feel secure and comfortable in a new place.

- **Waste Bags:** Be prepared to clean up after your Maltipoo, especially if you're traveling in places where leaving waste behind is against regulations.

- **Health Documents:** Many hotels and airlines require proof of your pet's health and vaccinations. It's a good idea to have a copy of your Maltipoo's vaccination record, health insurance, and your vet's contact information.

While it's important to keep your Maltipoo hydrated, especially during active travel, remember that dogs' bodies don't sweat the same way humans do. Instead, dogs primarily cool down by panting! So, if your Maltipoo is panting after an exciting hike, make sure they get plenty of water and rest.

Travel Arrangements

Depending on the length and nature of your trip, you may be traveling by car, train, or plane. Each mode of travel has its unique challenges and considerations.

Traveling by Car

If you're traveling by car, you have more control over the environment and can stop for breaks as needed. It's crucial to secure your Maltipoo for safety. A travel carrier or harness that attaches to a seat belt will help keep your Maltipoo secure.

Remember, you should never leave your Maltipoo alone in the car, especially in hot weather. The temperature inside a parked car can rise very quickly, leading to potentially fatal heat stroke.

Traveling by Train

Train travel policies vary, so it's essential to check with the train company about their pet policy before planning your journey. Some trains allow small dogs like Maltipoos in carriers, while others may not permit pets at all.

Traveling by Plane

When flying, small dogs like Maltipoos are often allowed in the cabin if they're in an airline-approved carrier that fits under the seat in front of you. It's crucial to check your airline's specific pet policy before booking your flight.

Air travel can be stressful for dogs, so it's important to make your Maltipoo as comfortable as possible. Line their carrier with a familiar blanket and add a few favorite toys. Try to exercise your Maltipoo before the flight so they're more likely to sleep. Avoid feeding them too close to the flight to prevent motion sickness.

> When flying with your Maltipoo, try to book direct flights when possible. This minimizes the amount of time your pet spends in potentially stressful environments like busy airports.

Selecting Pet-Friendly Accommodation

Researching and selecting pet-friendly accommodations is crucial. Websites like BringFido and PetsWelcome can help you find pet-friendly hotels, bed & breakfasts, and vacation rentals.

When you're booking, it's important to confirm their pet policy. Some places may have restrictions on the size or number of pets, additional charges for pets, or specific rules you'll need to follow during your stay.

Pet travel has become so popular that many places now offer pet amenities, such as doggy daycare, pet-friendly restaurants, and even dog spas. Your Maltipoo might just have as much vacation fun as you do!

Ensuring a Positive Travel Experience

Reducing Travel Stress

No matter how well-traveled your Maltipoo is, new environments can still cause stress. Here are some tips to help ease any anxiety:

- **Familiarity:** Bring items familiar to your Maltipoo, like their blanket, bed, toys, or treats.

- **Consistency:** Maintain your Maltipoo's regular feeding and walking schedule as much as possible.

- **Gradual Exposure:** Gradually expose your Maltipoo to travel experiences, like car rides, before embarking on long trips.

Exploring New Locations

Once you've reached your destination, take some time to familiarize your Maltipoo with their new environment. Start by letting them explore the immediate surroundings of your accommodation on a leash. Remember to provide plenty of praise and treats to build positive associations with the new place.

Check if there are local parks or walking paths where your Maltipoo can exercise and explore. Websites like DogFriendly can help you find pet-friendly parks, attractions, and restaurants in your destination.

In conclusion, with careful planning and preparation, traveling with your Maltipoo can be a rewarding experience that strengthens your bond and provides exciting new experiences for both of you. Whether you're exploring the great outdoors or relaxing in a cozy vacation rental, there's nothing quite like sharing the adventure with your furry best friend.

> "A journey is best measured in friends, rather than miles." - Tim Cahill, and your Maltipoo can be the best travel friend you could ask for!

CHAPTER 11

Connecting with the Maltipoo Community

Networking, Resources, and Advocacy

Whether you're a proud Maltipoo parent or looking to bring one into your life, being a part of the Maltipoo community can be both rewarding and informative. The Maltipoo community is an amalgamation of breed enthusiasts, experienced breeders, and Maltipoo owners, all sharing a common love for these adorable furballs. This chapter will guide you through the Maltipoo community's various aspects, how to network, how to utilize resources, and advocate for ethical Maltipoo ownership.

Joining the Maltipoo Community

Finding Local and Online Maltipoo Communities

The Internet makes it easier than ever to find and join local or global Maltipoo communities. Websites and social media platforms are fantastic places to start. Facebook groups, Instagram pages, and online forums dedicated to Maltipoos offer a platform to share experiences, ask questions, and learn from others.

> Social media platforms like Instagram have unique hashtags such as #Maltipoo, #MaltipooOfInstagram, and #MaltipooPuppy that can help you find and connect with other Maltipoo owners and enthusiasts.

Offline, you can look for local dog clubs or breed-specific meetups. Maltipoo-specific gatherings, often referred to as "Maltipoo meetups," are fun events where owners and their pets can socialize. These meetups can be found in many cities, and they're an excellent opportunity for your Maltipoo to play and interact with other dogs.

If you can't find a Maltipoo-specific meetup in your city, general small dog meetups can be equally beneficial. Websites like Meetup.com are useful for finding local dog meetups.

Navigating the Maltipoo Community

Understanding Community Etiquette

Online or offline, every community operates with certain unspoken rules or etiquettes. Here are some to keep in mind:

- **Respect Different Opinions:** Everyone may not share the same views about raising or training a Maltipoo. Respect differing opinions and avoid engaging in debates that might lead to conflicts.

- **Ask Open-Ended Questions:** When asking for advice, provide as much detail as possible and invite solutions rather than yes/no answers. This can help you gather a variety of perspectives.

- **Share Responsibly:** Be cautious about sharing advice yourself. Ensure any information you provide is accurate and beneficial to others in the community.

- **Remember Online Safety:** Be mindful of the personal information you share online. Avoid sharing specific locations or other sensitive information.

Leveraging Community Resources

Maltipoo communities are treasure troves of information and resources. Experienced Maltipoo owners can offer practical advice about behavioral challenges, grooming tips, diet recommendations, and more. Breeders or veterinary professionals within the community can provide expert advice on health-related questions.

Community members often share recommendations for products they've found useful, such as chew toys, grooming tools, or travel accessories.

> A study by the American Veterinary Medical Association found that people who had strong bonds with their pets also reported strong connections to their communities. The mutual love for pets can serve as a powerful social glue, fostering a sense of community spirit.

Communities also share local resources like the names of good veterinarians, dog-friendly parks, and pet stores that stock high-quality products.

In case of missing pets or emergencies, your community can provide immediate support.

Participating in Community Events

Participation in community events can deepen your connection with fellow Maltipoo enthusiasts. Whether it's a fun costume competition, a charity dog walk, or a grooming workshop, these events offer learning opportunities and foster a sense of camaraderie. They're also an excellent opportunity for your Maltipoo to socialize.

Advocating for Ethical Maltipoo Ownership and Breeding

Understanding Ethical Breeding Practices

Ethical breeding is at the heart of ensuring that Maltipoos are healthy and well-cared for. It includes practices like providing proper medical care for breeding dogs, ensuring suitable living conditions, and avoiding overbreeding.

Unfortunately, not all breeders follow these guidelines. Puppy mills, where dogs are bred repeatedly for profit without regard for their well-being, are sadly still a problem.

Promoting Ethical Breeding and Ownership

As a Maltipoo owner, you can promote ethical breeding and ownership in several ways:

- **Educate Yourself and Others:** Learn about ethical breeding practices and share this knowledge within your community. Encourage others to only support ethical breeders or consider adopting from rescue centers.

- **Support Responsible Breeders:** If you choose to buy a Maltipoo from a breeder, ensure they adhere to ethical breeding practices. They should provide appropriate medical care, socialization opportunities, and living conditions for their dogs.

- **Advocate for Adoption:** Many Maltipoos in shelters need loving homes. By choosing to adopt, you're giving a dog a second chance at happiness.

- **Report Unethical Practices:** If you encounter a breeder you believe is unethical or a puppy mill, report them to your local animal welfare organization.

Supporting Maltipoo Rescue and Adoption Initiatives

Maltipoo rescue organizations do commendable work in rescuing, rehabilitating, and rehoming Maltipoos. You can support these organizations in several ways:

- **Adopt a Maltipoo:** Consider adopting a Maltipoo from a rescue organization. Not only will you be giving a Maltipoo a loving home, but you'll also be making space for the organization to rescue another dog.

- **Donate:** Most rescue organizations operate on donations. Monetary contributions can help cover costs like medical care, shelter, and food.

- **Volunteer:** Rescue organizations often need volunteers for tasks like fostering, transporting dogs, or organizing events.

- **Spread the Word:** Use your platforms, both online and offline, to raise awareness about the work these organizations do.

As Charles Schulz, the creator of the Peanuts comic strip, once said, "Happiness is a warm puppy." By being a part of the Maltipoo community, not only do you enhance your happiness and that of your Maltipoo, but you also contribute to the broader happiness and well-being of Maltipoos everywhere.

CHAPTER 12

Maltipoo Grooming
Ensuring Your Pet Looks and Feels Their Best

Grooming is more than just keeping your Maltipoo pretty—it's about maintaining their health and comfort too. This chapter provides a comprehensive guide on managing the specific grooming needs of a Maltipoo, ensuring they both look and feel their best.

The Importance of Regular Grooming

Grooming is crucial for every dog breed, but for a Maltipoo, it holds an extra level of significance. Maltipoos possess a curly or wavy coat that is typically hypoallergenic. This means that it doesn't shed much, but also that it can mat and tangle easily. Regular grooming keeps their coat clean, manageable, and free of mats.

Moreover, grooming is not just about maintaining their coat. It also includes nail care, dental hygiene, and ear cleaning. Regular grooming practices will help you spot any abnormalities or early signs of health problems, such as skin irritations, ticks, or dental issues.

> Grooming your Maltipoo at home provides an excellent bonding opportunity. It also allows your pup to feel comfortable during grooming sessions since they are in a familiar environment with their trusted human.

Essential Grooming Tools for Your Maltipoo

Before delving into the specifics of Maltipoo grooming, let's discuss the essential tools you'll need:

- **Brush:** A slicker brush is perfect for Maltipoos as it can effectively remove mats and tangles.

- **Comb:** A steel comb with both wide and narrow teeth will help ensure a thoroughly detangled coat.

- **Shampoo and Conditioner:** Choose a product formulated for dogs, preferably one designed for hypoallergenic breeds or breeds with curly or wavy hair.

- **Nail Clippers or Grinder:** Nail care is crucial, and you can use either clippers or a grinder, depending on what your Maltipoo is more comfortable with.

- **Toothbrush and Toothpaste:** Special dog toothbrushes and toothpaste are available for maintaining your Maltipoo's oral health.

- **Ear Cleaning Solution:** For keeping your Maltipoo's ears clean, you'll need a dog-friendly ear cleaning solution.

- **Hair Clippers:** If you plan on trimming your

Maltipoo's hair at home, a quality pair of dog hair clippers will come in handy.

Step-by-Step Guide to Grooming Your Maltipoo

Step 1: Brushing Your Maltipoo

Brushing your Maltipoo's coat should be a daily routine. Regular brushing prevents the formation of mats, removes dirt and debris, and distributes natural skin oils through their coat, keeping it healthy and shiny.

Start by using a slicker brush to go over your Maltipoo's entire body. Make sure to be gentle and avoid pulling at any tangles or mats. If you come across a mat, use your fingers to try to loosen it before gently brushing it out.

Next, go over their coat with a steel comb to remove any remaining tangles. Make sure to comb all the way down to the skin—but be careful not to scratch or irritate the skin.

> Always brush and detangle your Maltipoo's coat before bathing them. Water can cause tangles and mats to tighten, making them more difficult to remove.

Step 2: Bathing Your Maltipoo

Maltipoos don't require frequent baths—once a month is usually enough unless they get particularly dirty or have a skin condition that requires more frequent bathing. Over-bathing can dry out their skin and coat.

Fill a tub or sink with warm (not hot) water, enough to reach your Maltipoo's knees. Wet their coat thoroughly, then apply dog shampoo, working it in with your fingers from head to tail. Remember to be careful around their eyes and ears.

Rinse thoroughly, ensuring all shampoo is removed, as any residue can irritate their skin. Follow up with a dog conditioner to keep their coat soft and manageable, then rinse again. After the bath, wrap your Maltipoo in a towel and gently pat them dry.

Step 3: Drying and Brushing Post-Bath

After patting your Maltipoo dry with a towel, you can use a hairdryer to finish the job. Make sure to use a low heat setting to avoid overheating or burning their skin.

Once your Maltipoo is completely dry, brush them again to remove any tangles caused by the bathing process.

Step 4: Nail Trimming

Nail care is crucial for your Maltipoo's comfort and health. Overgrown nails can cause discomfort and even affect your dog's gait, leading to skeletal problems. Depending on how quickly your Maltipoo's nails grow, you may need to trim them every 2-4 weeks.

If using nail clippers, make a swift, decisive cut to avoid splintering the nail. If you're using a grinder, apply it in short bursts to prevent overheating the nail. Be careful not to cut or grind into the quick, the sensitive inner part of the nail that contains blood vessels and nerves.

Step 5: Dental Care

Maltipoos, like all dogs, can develop dental problems if their teeth aren't regularly cared for. Aim to brush your Maltipoo's teeth daily or at least several times a week.

Use a dog toothbrush and dog toothpaste—never use human toothpaste, as it can be harmful to dogs. Gently brush their teeth in circular motions, paying attention to the gum line.

Step 6: Ear Cleaning

Check your Maltipoo's ears weekly for signs of irritation, infection, or parasites. A dog's ear canal is shaped like an "L," so don't insert anything deep into their ear. Instead, use a dog-friendly ear cleaning solution and gently clean the visible part of their inner ear with a cotton ball.

Step 7: Hair Trimming

Maltipoos require haircuts every 6–8 weeks. Whether you choose to do this at home or prefer a professional groomer depends on your comfort level and your Maltipoo's temperament. If you opt to trim at home, make sure to read up on the correct techniques to avoid any mishaps.

Recognizing and Preventing Common Grooming Issues

Grooming is usually a positive experience for your Maltipoo, but sometimes issues may arise. Here are common problems and tips on preventing them:

- **Matting:** This can be prevented with daily brushing and regular haircuts. If you encounter a mat, never try to cut it out with scissors, as it's easy to accidentally cut the skin. Instead, try to gently detangle it with your fingers and a brush or comb.

- **Dry Skin:** This can result from over-bathing or harsh shampoos. Always use a dog-friendly, gentle shampoo and follow up with a conditioner. If your Maltipoo's skin seems dry despite proper bathing practices, consult your vet.

- **Ear Infections:** Regular ear cleaning can help prevent these. If your Maltipoo seems to be scratching their ears a lot or if their ears look red or smell bad, consult your vet.

- **Nail Bleeding:** If you accidentally cut into the quick of your Maltipoo's nail, it can cause bleeding. Having a styptic powder on hand can quickly stop the bleeding. If you're not comfortable trimming their nails, consider a professional groomer or vet.

Making Grooming a Positive Experience for Your Maltipoo

Begin grooming practices early in your Maltipoo's life so they can get used to it. Always approach grooming with a calm and positive demeanor—your Maltipoo can sense your emotions.

Use positive reinforcement during grooming. Praise your Maltipoo, speak in a soft, reassuring voice, and offer treats. Never rush through the grooming process, as it can stress your Maltipoo.

> "Regular grooming sessions are a fantastic opportunity to bond with your pet and ensure their overall health. Make these moments enjoyable for both of you, filled with love, treats, and perhaps a bit of playful silliness," suggests professional groomer Linda Philips.

In conclusion, regular grooming is essential for keeping your Maltipoo looking and feeling their best. It might seem overwhelming at first, but with time, patience, and practice, it will become a normal and enjoyable part of your routine. Happy grooming!

CHAPTER 13

The Aging Maltipoo
Navigating the Golden Years

Just as the joy of raising a Maltipoo puppy can be profound, so can be the journey through their golden years. These latter years of your Maltipoo's life present unique challenges, but they also come with deep rewards: the comfort of companionship, the richness of shared experiences, and the understanding that comes from navigating life together.

This chapter will guide you through the physical and mental changes that your Maltipoo will experience as they age. We'll provide tips for maintaining their comfort, wellness, and happiness, and offer guidance on navigating end-of-life decisions compassionately and respectfully.

Understanding the Aging Process in Maltipoos

Physical Changes

As your Maltipoo ages, their physical condition will naturally begin to change.

> Small dogs like Maltipoos are often considered seniors when they reach 10-12 years, although many remain spry and healthy well beyond this milestone!

Here are some common physical changes you might observe:

- **Weight Changes:** Aging Maltipoos may gain or lose weight due to changes in metabolism or underlying health issues. Regular weight checks (every month) can help you catch any significant changes. A healthy weight range for a senior Maltipoo is typically 5-15 lbs (2.3-6.8 kg), but this can vary based on their individual size and build.

- **Coat Changes:** Your Maltipoo's lush coat may begin to thin or gray, particularly around the muzzle and eyes.

- **Mobility Issues:** Arthritis is common in older dogs and can lead to stiffness, difficulty climbing stairs, or a limp. Some Maltipoos may also experience a general slowing down in their movements.

- **Dental Issues:** Older Maltipoos can be prone to dental disease. Regular brushing and veterinary dental check-ups can help prevent or treat these issues.

- **Sense Changes:** Just like humans, Maltipoos' senses can dull with age. You might notice they don't hear your arrival as quickly as they used to, or they might need more coaxing to come for a meal, hinting at a reduced sense of smell.

Mental Changes

Aging can also bring changes to your Maltipoo's mental health. Cognitive Dysfunction Syndrome (CDS), similar to dementia in humans, can affect senior dogs. Signs of CDS can include disorientation, changes in sleep patterns, decreased interaction, house soiling, or changes in activity levels.

> If you notice significant behavioral changes in your senior Maltipoo, don't assume it's just "old age"—consult with your vet. Many conditions, including CDS, can be managed with the right care and treatment.

Caring for an Aging Maltipoo

Adjusted Diet and Exercise

As your Maltipoo ages, their nutritional and exercise needs will change.

Senior dogs often need fewer calories, as their metabolism slows down. However, their diet should still be rich in high-quality protein to maintain muscle mass, and have balanced amounts of fiber and fats. Your vet can help you adjust your Maltipoo's diet to their specific needs.

Regular, gentle exercise is crucial for keeping your senior Maltipoo fit and managing arthritis symptoms. Shorter, more frequent walks can be easier on their joints than long excursions.

Regular Vet Check-Ups

Annual veterinary check-ups are essential for all dogs, but for seniors, you might want to consider semi-annual visits. Regular vet visits can catch potential health issues early, such as heart disease, kidney disease, or cancer, which are more common in older dogs.

Comfortable Environment

Make sure your Maltipoo's environment caters to their changing needs. Orthopedic beds can provide joint support, while non-slip mats can help prevent slips and falls. If your Maltipoo has trouble jumping onto their favorite couch, consider a pet ramp or stairs.

Navigating End-of-Life Decisions

Discussing the end of life can be difficult, but it's essential to consider your Maltipoo's quality of life as they age. When they're no longer able to enjoy the things they once loved, or when discomfort or pain becomes unmanageable, you may need to consider end-of-life decisions.

Remember, it's okay to seek support. Reach out to your vet, a pet bereavement counselor, or a trusted person in your life as you navigate this difficult time.

Mourning Your Maltipoo

When the time comes to say goodbye to your Maltipoo, it's natural and healthy to grieve. Mourning is a deeply personal process, and there's no right or wrong way to go about it. Some people might find comfort in holding a small ceremony or creating a keepsake, such as a clay paw print or a photo album.

No matter how you choose to remember your Maltipoo, remember that it's okay to grieve and it's okay to seek support. You're not alone—there are many resources and communities available to help you through this difficult time.

In conclusion, navigating your Maltipoo's golden years can be a journey filled with mixed emotions. Yet, despite the challenges, it can also be a deeply rewarding phase, filled with shared comforts, slow-paced walks, and mutual understanding. Your Maltipoo has been a cherished companion throughout various life stages, and this final stage is no different. As always, they rely on your love, patience, and dedication to their well-being.

As American writer Dean Koontz once said, "Once you have had a wonderful dog, a life without one, is a life diminished." Even though the aging process can be challenging, it's all part of the rich tapestry of sharing your life with a Maltipoo—a journey that, despite its inevitable end, is filled with countless moments of joy, companionship, and love.

CHAPTER 14

Maltipoo Q&A
Common Questions and Concerns

As you embark on this wonderful journey of Maltipoo parenthood, you're likely to come across various questions and concerns. In this chapter, we'll address some of the most frequently asked questions about Maltipoos, their behavior, health, and overall care.

Remember, every Maltipoo is an individual with its unique quirks and traits. However, this guide will give you a general understanding of what to expect from your new furry friend.

Q1: How long does a Maltipoo live?

Typically, a Maltipoo lives between 12 to 16 years, given they receive proper care and a healthy lifestyle. Their lifespan is influenced by factors such as diet, exercise, preventative care, and genetics. It's also noteworthy that smaller dogs tend to live longer than larger breeds.

Did you know? The oldest known Maltipoo lived to be 20 years old!

Q2: How big will my Maltipoo get?

Maltipoos usually reach full size around the 6-8 months mark. The size of your Maltipoo as an adult depends on its parents. Typically, Maltipoos weigh between 5 to 20 pounds (2.3 to 9 kg) and stand about 8 to 14 inches (20 to 35 cm) tall at the shoulder.

Q3: Are Maltipoos good with children and other pets?

Yes, Maltipoos generally get along well with children and other pets. However, it's crucial to teach children how to interact appropriately with your Maltipoo to avoid unintentional injury due to their small size. Similarly, while Maltipoos can get along with other pets, proper introductions and supervised interactions are necessary to ensure harmonious relationships.

Did you know? Maltipoos are often used as therapy dogs due to their gentle and friendly nature!

Q4: How often should I groom my Maltipoo?

Maltipoos have hair, not fur, similar to their Poodle parent. This means they require regular grooming to keep their coats in top shape. Most Maltipoos need grooming every 4-6 weeks, depending on the length and condition of their coat. Daily brushing is also a good practice to prevent matting and tangles.

Q5: Do Maltipoos suffer from separation anxiety?

Maltipoos are known for their loving and affectionate nature, which can make them prone to separation anxiety if left alone for long periods. If your Maltipoo shows signs of distress when you're away, it's important to gradually acclimate them to your absence, create positive associations with alone time, and consider interactive toys or a pet sitter to keep them occupied.

Tip: Crate training from a young age can help provide a safe and comfortable space for your Maltipoo when you're not around.

Q6: What should I feed my Maltipoo?

Maltipoos thrive on high-quality dog food suitable for their size, age, and activity level. A balanced diet for a Maltipoo should consist of high-quality proteins, fats, carbohydrates, and micronutrients. Always consult your vet for personalized dietary advice.

> "A dog is what he eats – feed him like a king, and he'll treat you like his world." – Pet Nutritionist Claire Miller

Q7: How much exercise does my Maltipoo need?

Despite their small size, Maltipoos are energetic and enjoy regular exercise. Aim for about 30–60 minutes of physical activity per day. This can include walks, playtime, and mental stimulation activities like puzzle toys.

Q8: Are Maltipoos hypoallergenic?

No dog breed is 100% hypoallergenic, but Maltipoos are among the breeds less likely to trigger allergies. This is due to their Poodle parentage, which has a low-shedding coat. However, reactions vary from person to person, and it's always best to spend time with a Maltipoo before bringing one home if allergies are a concern.

Q9: Can Maltipoos be left alone during the day?

Maltipoos are companion dogs who thrive on human interaction. If left alone for extended periods, they may experience separation anxiety. If you have a full-time job, consider hiring a dog walker, enrolling your Maltipoo in a doggy daycare, or arranging for a friend or family member to spend time with them during the day.

Q10: How do I train my Maltipoo?

Maltipoos are intelligent and eager to please, making them quite trainable. Use positive reinforcement techniques such as treats, praise, and playtime. Be consistent, patient, and make sure to socialize your Maltipoo from a young age.

Remember, the bond between you and your Maltipoo thrives on understanding and love. As you continue to spend time together, the relationship will deepen, turning your Maltipoo from a pet into a family member.

> **Tip:** Maltipoos are known for their intelligence. Make training a fun and rewarding experience to capitalize on this!

Finally, while this guide answers many common queries, it's essential to maintain regular communication with your vet to address health-related questions. After all, our canine companions rely on us for their well-being, and it's our duty to ensure they lead a happy, healthy, and fulfilling life.

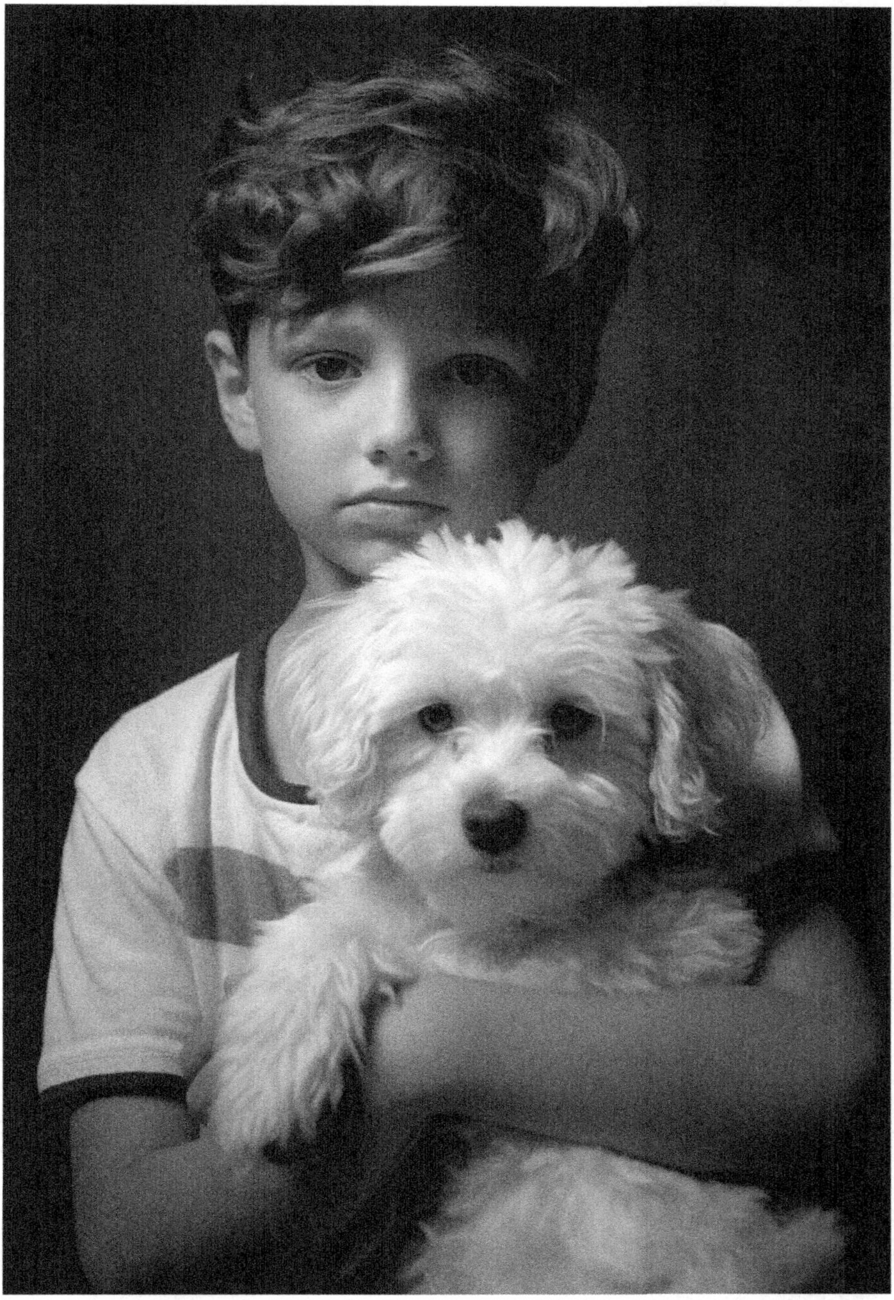

CHAPTER 15

Maltipoos and Kids/Other Pets
Ensuring Harmonious Relationships

Creating a harmonious home environment where Maltipoos, kids, and other pets coexist peacefully can seem like a daunting task. But it doesn't have to be. With the right guidance and strategies, you can foster positive interactions and prevent common issues. This chapter will help you navigate these relationships and teach kids to interact appropriately with your Maltipoo.

Introducing Your Maltipoo to Children

Maltipoos are generally known for their friendly and adaptable nature, making them great companions for families. However, it's essential to lay a solid foundation for positive interactions between your kids and the new family pet.

Preparation is Key

Before you introduce your Maltipoo to your children, take some time to educate them about the new family member's needs, temperament, and care. Teach them about the Maltipoo's small size and the need to handle the dog gently.

> "Education is the most powerful tool which you can use to change the world." – Nelson Mandela

The First Meeting

When introducing your Maltipoo to your children, ensure the environment is calm and quiet. A noisy, chaotic environment can stress the dog, leading to an unsuccessful first meeting.

Gentle Interaction

Teach your children to approach the Maltipoo gently and quietly, allowing the dog to sniff their hands first. Children should be encouraged to pet the Maltipoo softly, preferably on the back or chest, rather than reaching for the dog's face or tail.

Fun Fact: Dogs use their sense of smell to get to know their surroundings. Letting the Maltipoo sniff your child's hand allows the dog to 'introduce' itself!

Setting Boundaries

Establish clear rules for interacting with the Maltipoo. These might include no pulling on the dog's ears or tail, no disturbing the dog while it's eating or sleeping, and no shouting or running around the dog.

Introducing Your Maltipoo to Other Pets

Just like with kids, introducing your Maltipoo to other pets requires careful planning and patience. Remember, each pet is an individual with its unique personality and temperament.

Familiar Scent Introduction

Before your Maltipoo meets another pet face-to-face, let them become familiar with each other's scent. You can do this by exchanging blankets or toys between your Maltipoo and the other pet. This process can help reduce stress and make the first meeting smoother.

Neutral Ground Meeting

Arrange the first meeting on neutral ground, like a quiet park or a friend's yard. Neutral territory prevents any pet from feeling the need to protect their territory. Keep both pets on leashes for better control.

Gradual Integration

Allow the pets to see and sniff each other without any physical contact initially. Look for signs of stress or aggression, like growling, showing teeth, or raised fur. If all seems calm, let them interact under close supervision, ready to intervene if necessary.

Consistent Supervision

Until you're confident that your pets can get along without any issues, always supervise their interactions. It's also essential to provide separate spaces for each pet to retreat to if they feel stressed or need some alone time.

> "Patience is not about waiting, but the ability to keep a good attitude while waiting." – Joyce Meyer

Training Kids to Interact Appropriately with Your Maltipoo

Teaching kids to interact appropriately with your Maltipoo isn't just about the initial introduction. It's an ongoing process that involves reinforcing good behavior and correcting undesirable actions.

Reinforce Gentle Behavior

Praise and reward your child for interacting gently with the Maltipoo. This could be anything from a soft pat on the Maltipoo's back to speaking to the dog in a calm, quiet voice.

Correct Undesirable Actions

If you notice your child interacting roughly or disrespectfully with the Maltipoo, it's essential to correct the behavior immediately. Explain why the action was inappropriate and how they should behave instead.

Involve Kids in Care

Involving your children in taking care of the Maltipoo can help them understand the responsibility of owning a pet and develop empathy. They can assist with tasks like feeding, grooming, or training, under adult supervision.

Teach by Example

Remember, children often learn by example. Treat your Maltipoo with kindness, respect, and care, and your children will likely follow suit.

> **Did you know?** Empathy, responsibility, and respect are just a few of the many values children can learn from interacting with pets!

In conclusion, creating a harmonious home environment where your Maltipoo, kids, and other pets coexist happily is a fulfilling task. It takes patience, understanding, and consistent guidance. As time goes on, the bond between them will deepen, and you'll have a home filled with love, respect, and furry companionship. Always remember, the key is to teach everyone to respect each other's space, comfort, and needs. It might not be the easiest task, but it's definitely worth it!

Tip: Keep a close eye on your Maltipoo's body language when they're around kids or other pets. If they appear uncomfortable or stressed, it might be time for a break. As a responsible pet owner, it's crucial to ensure your Maltipoo's wellbeing at all times.

In the next chapter, we'll discuss the crucial topic of emergency preparedness for your Maltipoo, to ensure you're ready for any situation that may arise.

CHAPTER 16

Emergency Preparedness for Your Maltipoo

Emergencies are often unpredictable, but preparing ahead can help you react quickly and effectively. This chapter is dedicated to providing you with the knowledge and resources necessary to ensure your Maltipoo's safety during emergencies.

Recognizing Common Pet Emergencies

> "The art of medicine consists of amusing the patient while nature cures the disease." – Voltaire

Understanding common pet emergencies is the first step in preparing for unforeseen situations. While the best course of action is always to contact a veterinarian immediately, recognizing signs of distress can save precious time.

Respiratory Distress
Maltipoos, like any dog, can experience respiratory distress. Watch for signs like increased breathing rate, gasping for breath, excessive coughing, and blue or pale gums. These symptoms could indicate serious conditions like heart disease or a foreign object lodged in the throat.

Gastrointestinal Issues
Vomiting and diarrhea are common in dogs and can be due to various causes, including dietary indiscretion, poi-

soning, or illnesses. If your Maltipoo has persistent vomiting or diarrhea, especially if blood is present or they are also lethargic, this is an emergency.

Seizures

While not overly common in Maltipoos, seizures can occur due to underlying conditions like epilepsy or metabolic disorders. A seizure might look like uncontrollable shaking, loss of consciousness, or abnormal behavior like excessive drooling or paddling of the legs.

Trauma

Accidents can happen to even the most well-cared-for dogs. If your Maltipoo has been hit by a car, fallen from a height, or sustained an injury from a fight with another animal, they need immediate veterinary care.

Reacting to Common Pet Emergencies

The manner in which you respond to an emergency can significantly impact your Maltipoo's wellbeing. It's crucial to stay calm, move quickly, and take the right steps.

Create a Safety Plan

Create a plan of action for emergencies. This includes knowing the location and contact information of your nearest 24-hour emergency veterinary clinic and having a basic understanding of pet CPR.

Fact: A Maltipoo's normal heart rate can range from 70 to 120 beats per minute, depending on their size and activity level.

Seek Veterinary Care Immediately

In any emergency, the first step is to contact your veterinarian or the nearest emergency veterinary clinic. They can provide guidance over the phone and prepare for your arrival.

Handle with Care

Injured or sick pets might behave unpredictably due to fear or pain. When handling your Maltipoo during an emergency, move slowly, use a soft voice, and if necessary, consider muzzling them to prevent bites.

Transport Safely

Use a carrier, a box, or a blanket to transport your Maltipoo to the vet. This reduces the risk of further injury and can provide some comfort to your pet.

Knowing When to Seek Emergency Veterinary Care

Sometimes it's difficult to discern a minor health issue from a severe emergency. Here are some circumstances where it's essential to seek emergency veterinary care:

- Your Maltipoo has been involved in a traumatic incident, like being hit by a vehicle or falling from a significant height.

- You notice signs of extreme discomfort, like persistent vomiting, bloody diarrhea, difficulty breathing, or inability to urinate.

- Your Maltipoo is experiencing a seizure, especially if it's their first seizure or it lasts more than a few minutes.

- Your Maltipoo is unable to stand, appears disoriented, or is experiencing a loss of balance.

- You suspect poisoning, such as ingestion of toxic

foods, chemicals, or plants.

Tip: Always keep any potentially toxic substances out of your Maltipoo's reach. This includes certain foods like chocolate, xylitol (a sweetener often found in sugar-free products), grapes, and raisins, as well as medications and household chemicals.

Basic First Aid for Pets

While first aid is not a substitute for veterinary care, it can be helpful in managing your Maltipoo's condition until you can get them professional help.

- **Cuts and Wounds:** If your Maltipoo has a small, superficial wound, clean it with warm water and mild soap. Apply a pet-safe antiseptic and cover the wound with a clean cloth or bandage. For deep wounds, apply a clean cloth to the area and apply pressure to stop bleeding.

- **Choking:** If your Maltipoo is choking, try to keep

them calm and look into their mouth for the obstruction. If you can see and easily reach the item without being bitten, gently try to remove it with tweezers. If you can't remove the item or your Maltipoo collapses, rush them to the vet while performing chest compressions.

- **Heatstroke:** Maltipoos are particularly prone to heatstroke. If your Maltipoo shows signs like excessive panting, drooling, reddened gums, or collapse, move them to a cooler area immediately. Apply cool (not cold) water to their body, especially the head and neck. Do not use ice or ice-cold water as this can worsen the situation. Take them to the vet immediately.

- **Poisoning:** If you suspect your Maltipoo has ingested something toxic, contact your vet or the Pet Poison Helpline (855-764-7661) immediately. Try to identify what your Maltipoo has ingested, as this can assist in treatment.

Did you know? The Pet Poison Helpline can provide immediate, expert advice on poisoning in pets.

Maintaining an Emergency Kit

An emergency kit is an essential tool in pet safety. Some basic items to include in your Maltipoo's emergency kit are:
- Bandages and gauze
- Tweezers
- A digital thermometer (a dog's normal body temperature should be between 100.5°F and 102.5°F or 38.1°C to 39.2°C)
- Hydrogen peroxide (can induce vomiting in case of poisoning, but only use when directed by a professional)
- A blanket
- A leash and muzzle
- Contact information for your vet and the nearest emergency clinic
- A current photo of your Maltipoo, in case they get lost
- A copy of your Maltipoo's medical records

Remember, being prepared for an emergency can make a huge difference in the outcome. Although it's something we never want to consider, having the knowledge and resources to act quickly can save your Maltipoo's life. In the end, the most important thing is to provide your Maltipoo with a safe, loving environment and a lifetime of happiness.

Afterword

As we conclude "The Maltipoo Method: A Guide to Successful Dog Ownership," I hope you feel well-prepared and excited to embark on your incredible journey with your Maltipoo. We've covered a broad spectrum of topics, from selecting your new best friend to ensuring their health and happiness throughout their life. My goal has been to provide a thorough, engaging, and enjoyable guide to aid you in becoming the best possible Maltipoo owner.

My Cavapoo, Isabel, is a constant source of inspiration and joy in my life, and I am confident your Maltipoo will offer the same for you. With the experiences shared in this book and the knowledge of veterinarians, cynologists, and canine behavior specialists, you should be able to forge a close bond with your Maltipoo while navigating the challenges and rewards of dog ownership.

Remember that love, patience, and consistency are the foundations of a successful relationship with your Maltipoo. These principles will accompany you as you encounter new challenges, share experiences, and grow together.

As you journey with your Maltipoo, always consider the broader community. Clubs, organizations, and other Maltipoo enthusiasts can offer support, friendship, and camaraderie. Share your experiences, learn from others, and continue to explore the fascinating world of Maltipoos.

I am grateful for the opportunity to share my love for Maltipoos with you and wish you and your pet a lifetime of joy, amusement, and companionship. Remember to cherish each moment as the years pass swiftly, and each day offers new opportunities for growth, learning, and love.

Thank you for joining me on this incredible journey. May "The Maltipoo Method" serve as your beacon and trusted resource throughout your journey with your beloved companion.

Sincerely,
Gus Tales & Isabel the Cavapoo

Printed in Great Britain
by Amazon